Y0-AQW-263

TENNIS
It's a
Mental Game

"Tennis-It's A Mental Game," by Paul Bundock Steel. ISBN 978-1-60264-443-4 (softcover); 978-1-60264-444-1 (ebook).

Published 2009 by Virtualbookworm.com Publishing Inc., P.O. Box 9949, College Station, TX 77842, US. ©2009, Paul Bundock Steel. All rights reserved. No part of this publication may be reproduced, stored in a retrieval system, or transmitted in any form or by any means, electronic, mechanical, recording or otherwise, without the prior written permission of Paul Bundock Steel.

Manufactured in the United States of America.

CONTENTS

PREFACE

Hi! My name is Paul and I have been playing tennis for about 17 years. I had long thought about writing a book on the mental side of the game which was a reflection of my own experiences on the court. It was based on the feeling that, for many years, I was unable to produce my best tennis in matches due to the pressure. I had always felt I lacked the mental toughness which can make the difference between winning and losing and decided one day, after much consideration, to write about it.

It is true to say that I am not a professional tennis coach — nor do I have any titles to my name — and so, therefore, cannot talk about the technical side of the game. I do, however, have experience in playing in matches and in the different situations that matches have provided me with and have used this to gain greater knowledge.

This book is mainly aimed at club players who are happy with their technique, even if it is unorthodox, but who are unable to produce the tennis they know they are capable of, especially when it matters.

I believe that the mind is key to unlocking our natural potential and, therefore, we should look at it in far greater depth, learning to understand how it works and using its sublime powers to our advantage.

In short, I hope that this book is an engaging read, that it will give you a greater understanding of what goes on in our minds and that it helps you to find a solution to your mental frailty.

INTRODUCTION

"It's a funny old game!" Isn't that what Jimmy Greaves said about football? I suppose you could say the same about tennis. I'm sure I've heard people say that in the past and I'm sure that generations to come will say the same in the future. Indeed, you could say that about any sport. For all you sports people reading this, I bet you can think of a time when it seemed easy and everything you touched turned to gold. And I bet you can think of a time when the opposite was true. Far more frequently I should imagine. Well, the same happens in tennis. Most tennis players would agree that at some stage they have played flawless tennis where everything was effortless and the feel for the shot and timing was all there. In tennis terms this is called 'in the zone'. And no doubt they would agree that there are those other times when they feel like they are trudging through mud, when the harder they try, the worse it gets. And during these times they would probably admit that luck seemed to go against them just when they needed all the help they could get.

Of course, when you are playing well, the opposite is true. And this is one of the areas that I want to explore in the book. For it never ceases to amaze me that every time I play well, luck goes with me. But when I play badly, luck goes against me. It is not the case some of the time, this is what happens every time. And this is not just true of myself; it is true of others as well. I have watched people when they are playing well; their shot would clip the top of the net and fall on their opponent's side. If they were not playing well, then the ball would fall on their side. I have often asked myself the question 'why does this always happen?' For it certainly doesn't seem fair. And it certainly doesn't seem to follow the laws of probability.

Through the book I will briefly cover the mechanics of tennis, but my main concern is dealing with the mental side of the game. About what goes on in our minds when we are playing. Tennis is like a game of chess. It's about building each point up, balancing aggression with defense, and being the first player to get the mental upper hand.

I shall be delving even deeper than this, though, and taking the book to where no other tennis book has gone before. I want to prove to you that tennis is spiritual. I shall explain that something extraordinary happens when we play well or even when we are relaxed and happy, and to discuss my theory as to why lady luck comes our way when we are 'in the zone'.

I shall also be looking at memory recall. This is about how our brain remembers how to hit a shot using the same motion automatically each time, and how this is compromised in certain situations.

In the penultimate chapter I will be looking at pressure, how we recognise it during a match and how we can deal with it. For I believe that you can't instantly make yourself play well, but I do believe you can train yourself to play better under pressure.

And in the last chapter I shall be concentrating on tactics and having an overall game plan. I will touch on different things we can do, from bluffing our opponent to having as many as three different game plans, and that by having a variety of shots will keep our opponent guessing.

One of the several reasons why I wrote this book was to help myself become stronger mentally. I hope that it will help you too.

CHAPTER 1
It's all about winning

Winning a tennis match is a great feeling. It is a just reward for all the effort and training that you have put in. But is winning the most important thing? It has been said, 'It's the taking part that counts'. But try telling that to somebody who has just lost a match. Of course, everybody likes to win and certainly plays to win. But sometimes we can try too hard to win and end up shooting ourselves in the foot. The problem can start when the need to win boils over from fear of losing. What happens is that we constrict our minds into thinking that we must win and therefore placing a lot of pressure on ourselves. This pressure that we have placed on ourselves can have an adverse effect on us and on our game. Our game starts to fall apart and we probably end up losing, which is the exact opposite of what we were trying to achieve in the first place.

When I first played tennis and for a few years leading on from there, I would tell myself that I was going to win this tennis match. It was a very positive statement with the intent of carrying out that statement. But deep down I had doubts about this. Because now I had to fulfill this command that I had given myself; it was placing me under undue pressure. This pressure stopped me from playing the way I would have liked and so the only option was to play safe. This meant that I safeguarded the match by cutting out the errors and this resulted in me pushing at the ball rather than hitting it. My low confidence was seriously affecting the way I hit the ball and the timing of the shot. As I was unhappy with the way I was playing and with the fact that I was losing, I would try to be more positive by going for an aggressive shot. Unfortunately, I had lost so much confidence in my own ability that I would almost certainly make an error. By now I was in a quandary, not sure what to do for the best. I started getting frustrated and giving off negative body language. This was food and drink for my opponent. From then on I may as well have started tanking because I no longer cared. But strangely I started to play a bit better. It wasn't enough to save the match, but it did make me think, 'why couldn't I do that earlier'?'

When I told myself I was going to win the match, I didn't give as much thought about the journey, i.e. the tennis, as I did about the end result. And so this brings me to the main point. 'It is neither the winning nor the taking part that counts, but that you enjoy it'. And this can be achieved by concentrating on performance or playing well rather than winning. When we concentrate on winning, we are placing all our eggs into one basket. It is as if the enjoyment of winning outweighs the enjoyment of playing. Do we look upon winning as a single entity, so that no matter how well or badly we have played, as long as we have won, then we are happy? I have known players who have told me that they played badly and yet still won. But rather than feeling elated, although they might have had some sense of relief, they felt as though they did not earn the victory and also felt dissatisfied with their own performance. For I believe that sometimes the journey can be more important than the end result.

Do you remember one of the classic episodes of 'Only Fools and Horses' when Del Boy and Rodney came across a watch and were advised to hand it in to an auction? The story goes that Raquel (Del's partner) invited her parents over for a meal. Her father, who had one glass of wine too many, thought he shouldn't drive home and so asked if they could both stay the night. The next morning, Raquel's dad, Del and Rodney go down to the garage where Del starts looking through some of his gear. On the previous day, Del had come across this watch and chucked it into a box believing it was worthless. Raquel's dad found the watch in the box,; picked it up and realised it was made by a famous marine watchmaker. He knew that only three of these were ever made and only two were ever accounted for. The dad said that this could be worth quite a bit of money and should be put up for auction. And so Del and Rodney took the watch to an auction to see how much they could get for it. As the bidding started, the value went up and up and up, and when a value of £50,000 was announced, Rodney crashed to the ground in disbelief. But the bidding hadn't finished and it still kept soaring with Del looking on in sheer amazement and disbelief. The bidding finally stopped at a cool £5,000,000 and Del joined Rodney on the floor. The Trotters were now millionaires and their ecstasy was on display for all to see. With the money they bought a new house and a Rolls Royce plus a motor cruise boat for Uncle Albert. Many weeks later, after the initial euphoria had subsided a little; Del admitted that he missed the buzz from wheeling and dealing when setting up his gear and the striving towards one day becoming rich or at least comfortable. Unfortunately, in the next episode they lost all their money after the shares they invested their money in crashed.

The moral of this story is that the actual act of aspiring or striving towards our dream or goal can be of greater significance in our lives and in helping us to identify who we are than in reaching that final goal itself. Put simply, the actual act of striving can often be more important than what we are striving for. There is a need in all of us to strive towards something. This act alone brings us some degree of self-worth and self-esteem. This matter can be applied to tennis as well. When we are thinking about winning, our mind is focusing on what comes afterwards i.e. the end result, rather than what comes before i.e. the tennis match itself.

Sometimes we cannot escape the feelings of pressure and I shall be looking at how we can overcome that later in the book. But wherever possible we want to unburden ourselves of this pressure. When I play a tennis match now I tell myself, 'I don't have to win this match' and this takes a whole weight off my shoulders. Deep down I still want to win, but now I have transferred my focus onto playing well rather than worrying about winning, as this is likely to make me nervous and therefore play too carefully or tentatively.

So now that I have focused my attention away from winning, I should be more relaxed and therefore happier. Now that I feel relaxed, I automatically start to play better. And now that I am playing well, I begin to feel good about my game and myself. I have now entered a virtuous circle where one feeds off the other. Before I was playing under the weight of expectancy or the need to win, which was manifesting itself as pressure and squeezing out the confidence in me. I was no longer enjoying my tennis and playing under the vain hope that my opponent would make all the mistakes, which meant that my mental state was riddled with negativity. Really, I did not deserve to win the match, as my thinking was all wrong. But now my thoughts are much more positive as I have been loosened from the chains of having to win. There is now a feeling of freedom, which is reflected in the way I am playing. This freedom will give birth to creativity, which will allow me to go for my shots and even to experiment with new ones with no fear of making a mistake. This freedom comes from being carefree and will give you a sense of a wider margin of error when playing your shots.

When you are a novice and just getting to grips with the game, a lot can be taken from inspiration. When I first started playing, my inspiration came from watching the top players on TV. I would watch my favourite players, see the way they hit their best shots and then do a re-enactment of their motion when playing a particular shot. I would take the serve and forehand of Pete Sampras, the backhand of Michael Stich or Boris Becker and the volley, especially the backhand volley, of Stefan Edberg. This was back in the early nineties when they were all in the top ten, and I can say that they helped me to fall in love with the game and to develop some shots. This also helped me to achieve what I have just been talking about: to focus my attention on playing well by trying to emulate their style or technique. Ivan Lendl talked about this in a video he brought out some years ago and showed that by watching and memorising shots of great players can help you to improve your technique through the process of visualisation. This is a very powerful tool to use because to the beholder the technical beauty of each shot adds a sense of beauty to the game and motivates the person watching to emulate that beauty on court.

Whilst you have been reading through this, I hope you have not felt that I am advocating that we should be shy of winning. Winning is very important but it is not the be-all and end-all. I believe that at club level it is even more important to enjoy your tennis and to stay healthy. By giving yourself the best chance of playing well, you will also be giving yourself the best chance of winning. If we shift our focus onto playing well, we will enjoy our tennis more and have greater confidence to play better tennis. This will help us to win more matches and we will feel as though we would have earned the victory all the more.

So, to summarise, I think it helps to focus your attention on playing well rather than winning and allow the winning to take care of itself. For, generally speaking, you cannot have the latter if you don't have the former.

CHAPTER 2
What are the causes of effortless play?

We have just seen from the previous chapter that when we free ourselves from pressure, we generally become more relaxed. When we relax, our quality of play starts to go up. If we can maintain a good level of play for any length of time, it is possible for us to play to our full natural potential. When this happens, we slip into what in tennis terms is called 'in the zone'. This is a wonderful feeling because everything you do becomes effortless. During this time your senses become sharper, your timing improves and you just seem to have more time to play your shots. Suddenly everything is so easy, as if you don't have to try. It is almost as if you have been taken over by a greater power that has put you in total control of the game. And because your senses are sharper you can pick up things quicker and therefore prepare earlier on your shot.

If you have ever listened to the commentary of a tennis match, I'm sure you've heard the commentator say that one of the players seems to have all the time in the world to play his shots, never looks rushed and is timing the ball so well. The other player by contrast, he says, looks rushed; his footwork is all over the place and has just dropped his serve again. I'm pretty sure from that description that the first player is probably 'in the zone' and the other player certainly isn't.

When a tennis player reaches this peak of play, the game suddenly becomes easy and uncomplicated. But generally speaking, we will have no control over when it happens, for we cannot make it happen. But it is more likely to happen if we are relaxed, enjoying our tennis and free of pressure.

As well as tennis, one of my other hobbies is building models. I revel in building the model as accurately as possible and to the minutest detail. Obviously, I require a lot of patience and concentration. But if my focus and concentration become really deep over a period of time and I become absorbed by it, I become completely detached from everything else around me. When I eventually step away and become conscious of myself again, all of my senses seem sharper and my whole being feels like it is on a higher level. It is as if my body is a temple. This is the model world's version of being 'in the zone'. Again, this level of awareness cannot be brought about simply by willing it. For it is as with sleep: best found unsought. And as with tennis, we don't acquire the end result by concentrating on it, but rather by concentrating on that which leads us to it.

When we are playing well in tennis, something happens, as it does in all other sports; we usually get a piece of lady luck thrown in for good measure. But the question that has always got me going is, 'why does the person who is playing well have the luck as well?' One of the reasons why I wrote this book was to explore this and to possibly come up with an answer to this question. You would have thought it would be much fairer if the opposite were true. I know that when I am having a really off day and everything seems to be going against me, I could really do with a bit of luck to get me out of this hole. To make me feel that the Gods aren't totally against me.

This luck most readily happens when we are 'in the zone' and playing effortless tennis. During this time we are playing carefree and may go a little way to explaining why luck would smile on us. After all, the motto that the S.A.S. adopt is, 'he who dares wins'. I know that when I am playing really well, the luck that I receive will usually come in the form of clipping the top of the net and falling onto my opponent's side. It won't necessarily happen at the most crucial time of the match, but it will happen sometime during the course of the match. Another piece of luck would be hitting the baseline or another line, probably from a lob where the intentions was not to hit the line at all. The margin of error was far too small. And all of this luck that I received would probably make my opponent feel like giving up.

So could we solve the unfairness of luck by looking at the theory of probability? Some people would say that luck would even itself out over the course of the match. That if one player has had two pieces of luck then the opposition should also experience two examples of luck before the match is concluded. The theory of probability works on the chances of something happening that constitutes luck, for example, the ball clipping the top of the net. To get a percentage of the likelihood of this happening, we would have to play the ball over the net many times, then divide the number of times the ball hits the net by the total number of balls hit. The problem is every time you experiment by hitting the ball over the net, say 200 times, you would very likely get a different result. And what if you tried to aim for the top of the net with every shot? You would probably have half the balls landing straight into the net. This all seems very inconclusive and really, it cannot be measured.

But could it be explained by looking at people who are considered lucky. Perhaps those people who receive the luck on the court are just born lucky. Research into answering the question, 'are some people born lucky?' found that this is not the case. The leading researcher of the study on luck and good fortune is Richard Wiseman who is a psychologist at the University of Hertfordshire. He says that lucky people generate their own good fortune via four basic principles. They have the ability to spot chance opportunities, make lucky decisions by listening to their intuition, create self-fulfilling prophesies via positive expectations, and adopt a resilient attitude that transforms bad luck into good. He also states that unlucky people are generally much more tense and anxious than lucky people, and this anxiety disrupts their ability to notice the unexpected.

A few years ago, an experiment was carried out whereby both lucky and unlucky people were given a rundown of a traumatic event. They had to imagine walking into a bank and suddenly a bank raider comes in and shoots them in the arm. The unlucky people were asked first how they felt. They basically said that they were unlucky and were in the wrong place at the wrong time. The lucky people said that they were lucky to have been shot in the arm and not anywhere else. It could have been so much worse. It is interesting to see the contrast in responses between the people considered as lucky and those considered as unlucky.

It definitely seems that lucky people have a much more positive outlook on life and are generally more relaxed and open to new opportunities. These people seem to be in the same frame of mind as those who receive the luck on the tennis court. But the luck that people create in their own lives is not really luck, but a positive attitude towards things where they see the glass as half full rather than half empty. Whereas, the luck that I am talking about on court, is completely random and outside the intention of the player. So if it cannot be explained by the previous two examples, perhaps something bigger is its cause.

I'm sure we have all at some time woken up in the middle of the night completely wide - awake. As we lie there, thoughts just start drifting into our minds. They may be thoughts from the previous day or something else completely different. But suddenly, everything becomes crystal clear, and the problem you may have been agonising over has been unravelled and now makes sense. This has happened because we suddenly possess a much greater insight into whatever we are thinking about. You see, as we have lost the stimulus and conscious thought processing that bombards us during the day, our minds are completely clear and free from the blockages that stop it flowing. I believe that when we have reached this state of awareness, we have sunk below the level of the conscious mind and are tapping into the peripheral zones of the subconscious mind. We are now in a meditative state similar to what I was explaining earlier when I was deeply absorbed by the model and had come away with my mind, body and soul revived. It is true that when we are very relaxed, we definitely can attain a higher level of awareness.

I am in no doubt that many musicians are aware of this fact. Some have been known to write their music between the hours of 11 p.m. and 4 a.m. when they feel they are most creative, or others who wake in the early hours, suddenly find that a series of notes or a new melody has drifted into their mind, so they jot it down before it is lost. They, like us, have tapped into a deeper sense of self. But what I am about to say now may seem far-fetched, but I am convinced it is the truth. For when we possess this crystal- clear thinking and our whole being is in a higher state of conscious-ness, we have tuned into ourselves and are at one with ourselves. But even more than this, I believe that when this happens, we become tuned into the powers of the universe. This is a very natural process and we are not aware of it. Indeed, many Eastern philosophies such as Taoism look at centering oneself whereby the powers of the ordered creation can flow into us so that we become one with them. But all human beings have this ability because we are receptors; we take in everything in the physical universe through our senses. But we are also spiritual beings and therefore can become receptive to the spiritual universe.

In the music world, when we think of Mozart, we think of a genius. He wrote some truly wonderful pieces of music. But I believe this music already existed long before Mozart was born. Maybe it has always existed. These wavelengths of sound have been drifting through the universe forever, and a little Mr. Mozart somehow tuned into these wavelengths and became the medium to which he brought them into the world. Basically, he was a receptor, just as a radio is a medium that acts as a receptor to pick up radio waves.

When we play tennis and attain a level where we are playing effortlessly, we are drawing on the powers that exist all around us subconsciously, without realising it. For when we are in this zone, the tennis racket feels like an extension of our arm rather than an alien object as it does when we are playing badly. This is also when we hit a shot and say, "how did I do that?". When we are aligned with the ordered cosmos, the natural potential that exists in all of us starts to shine through. And this may be a clue as to why we get lady luck falling on our side of the net when we are playing effortlessly. For this is how we are meant to live, being at one with ourselves, our fellow human beings and with all created things. This includes what we can see, the physical universe, and what we can't see, the spiritual universe. The physical universe is bound by the laws of physics and by time. But the spiritual universe is in another dimension where time, as we know it does not exist and the laws of physics no longer apply. The physical universe will one day end, but the spiritual universe has no end and it is where all things are possible.

The spiritual universe has a number of laws that are set for all that is spiritual. When we tune into the spiritual, although we are still bound by the physical laws such as gravity, we are obeying the spiritual laws. Although, when we have an out-of- body experience or a near death experience we may temporarily be free from the physical laws. But when we tap into the spiritual laws which are made up of infinite freedom, and wisdom and insight, we tap into the realm where miracles are commonplace. And when we have tuned into this realm, it can use us as a medium through which it can flow into this world in order to affect it. Because this realm has a far greater power than that which we can see, it can override the laws of this world and make something happen which to us appears as luck. When we hear about miracles, the same process is happening but on a much bigger scale, because it changes the life of an individual.

When we are nervous and are playing poor tennis, we are closed off from this realm, from the spiritual and are bound by this world with all its limitations. But when we are playing effortless tennis we are tuning into this infinite power, where there are no limits and where everything is possible. And this happens because of how we have been made. All of us have an energy field around us, which expands and contracts depending on how we feel. When we are unhappy, especially if we are experiencing fear, our whole energy field collapses in on itself and closes off the outside world. This is the body's way of shutting out the world when it becomes a danger to our existence. This energy field has now closed down, and is no longer able to connect with the spiritual wavelengths around it and is completely shut off from them. But when we are relaxed and happy, our energy field opens up and we are once more open to receiving the various wavelengths of energy around us.

It is a wonderful feeling when we aspire to play effortless tennis. It is indeed a very natural thing and will happen of its own accord. Therefore, you cannot force it or make it happen. But when it does you should take full advantage because being 'in the zone' can slip away as quickly as it came about. But more often than not, we will not play at this level. Indeed, in a match we are more likely to be playing under some degree of pressure. But what is pressure? And how can we recognise the symptoms that manifest themselves in a tennis match? Let's take a closer look.

CHAPTER 3
What is pressure?

For many players it is tough to play well under pressure. But what is pressure in relation to tennis? Perhaps it is when we have to win the next point or telling ourselves to hit a big shot when we don't feel confident, or perhaps it is when our opponent is giving us the run around and making us hit the shots we don't particularly want to play. It is usually when there is a lot at stake and therefore makes us feel nervous. When we feel pressure, our minds become constricted, which adversely affects our bodies and therefore our tennis. We become stiff and lack the freedom and creativity necessary for good play. At this stage, you certainly aren't tuned into the spiritual powers and luck will probably go against you as well.

I want to tell you a story about something that happened to me one day at school. It was in an English lesson and the teacher asked every pupil to talk about the book he had been reading as homework. Each pupil in turn came and stood in front of the class, spoke about the lead character and went on to explain the story so far. Well! I can tell you I was very nervous and whilst another pupil was talking, I flicked through the book desperately trying to think of something to say. When it came to my turn, I stood up in front of the class, which was only a small class, maybe 10 people. I started off by saying the book was called _____. It's about a boy named _____. He lived in the forest. He err! He err! Err! I was stuck and I began to flick through the pages to find any clues. This carried on for about a minute or so. The teacher, who could obviously see that I was struggling, asked me to take the book and go and stand in a corner of the classroom for about three minutes whilst another pupil spoke. By now I felt pretty bad. I began to flick through the pages again and thought to myself, "what the hell am I going to say". With feelings of terror, I knew I had to say something. Moments later the teacher called me back in front of the class and I started off in the same way as before. I got to about the same point and the same thing happened. I had a mental block and I couldn't for the life of me continue on. Worse was to come. As my body froze, I began to twiddle all my fingers uncontrollably. But I could not stop it. As I looked around the class, other pupils were pulling faces and making fun out of my inadequacy and foolishness. I continued to twiddle my fingers for what seemed like eternity, but I could not stop it. I had no control of my body whatsoever. My mind and body were paralysed by sheer embarrassment and indeed by fear. This was pressure in the extreme. Parts of my brain just seemed to shut down. I can honestly say I have never felt so small or degraded in my whole life. It was humiliating. But this is what pressure can do. It can paralyse our brain and stop it from sending the signals necessary for required movement. You hear of people who get frozen by fear, well I think that is what happened to me that day and it was rather unpleasant.

Pressure, of course, affects all of us at some point and tennis players are no exception. Of all the top players of recent years, none could seem to deal with pressure better than Pete Sampras. During an interview he was asked, "how do you deal with pressure?"? Pete answered by saying, and I quote, "I don't look upon it as pressure, but as an opportunity". He was referring to Wimbledon 2000, when he was going for a record 13th Grand Slam title. I believe this is a mature and positive way of dealing with pressure and may actually relieve those feelings we get. I think this attitude helps you to shift your focus and may well be worth cultivating the next time you feel under pressure in a tennis match.

But what happened to me at school can be explained in technical terms. When we face danger of any kind, our bodies will go into what is called the fight or flight response. This is part of the body's defence mechanism and will instinct-ively make the decision on whether to attack or run away, depending on the danger. In either case, the body produces a number of hormonal changes including an injection of adrenalin, whose purpose is to prepare the body for vigorous emergency action. During this time, food cannot be digested, causing a feeling of churning or butterflies in the stomach that can bring about nausea. Stored up fat and glucose are released into the bloodstream as fuel for the muscles. More oxygen is then required to burn off the fuel to produce energy and so breathing increases or becomes heavier. The blood carries the oxygen and fuel to the muscles in order to do their work but in this time of danger, they need more energy at a faster rate and so the heart beats faster to speed up the fuel- carrying blood that the muscles so desperately need. As the body begins to heat up due to the increased activity, it produces sweat to keep it cool and stop it from overheating. As all this is happening in the body, there are two important changes taking place. Firstly, the body's reflexes are speeded up and so is the thinking, which is why some people experience racing thoughts. Secondly, the blood supply to the frontal parts of the brain that control reasoning is reduced whilst it is increased to the brain stem, which is the more primitive side of the brain where instinctive reactions are controlled. This is why some people do things in the heat of the moment that they later regret.

In the infancy of man's development going back thousands of years, this is how he would react when faced with danger. But modern man living in the 21st century has been conditioned to suppress these symptoms, as to act out the fight or flight response would be inappropriate in our civil society.

With the situation I found myself in at school, I had all the symptoms of the fight or flight response but was not allowed to act on them. I wasn't allowed to pick a fight with the teacher but I also wasn't allowed to simply walk out of the class either. The only other instinct the body had left was to freeze. This is what can happen when there is a feeling of utter helplessness or fear. When we freeze, a neuro-muscular holding pattern is created that tenses the muscles in our body. The energy that is created from this is stored as 'body memory'. If the same traumatic event unfolds again, our memory recall will produce the same response of immobilising the body or whatever response the body would produce if the same traumatic event reoccurs. This is what happens in times of grave danger or when we feel threatened. But even when we are under a little bit of pressure, our minds and bodies can still be affected.

No matter whether we are in a relaxed state or under pressure, our brains are constantly sending out signals to our muscles and other organs to create determined movements. This happens whether we are thinking consciously or sub-consciously. These signals are made up of electrical messages that travel from the brain, via the nervous system, to the particular part of the body that requires movement. When we are under pressure, the brain produces a chemical that slows down the flow of these signals that travel from nerve ending to nerve ending. These signals, therefore, become fragmented and so the messages that were sent out may not arrive at their intended destination. That part of the brain that should have been activated to carry out a part of the overall message has been temporarily shut down. This explains why some people become forgetful or don't take in information very well under pressure.

This pressure or any kind of pressure that we do not relish can manifest itself as stress. If this stress is allowed to build up and go unchecked, then it can begin to have an adverse effect on our health. This stress is constantly re-producing the fight or flight responses in our bodies and therefore are being bombarded by chemicals such as adrenalin, which over a period of time will weaken our bodies. A good example of this is those who worked at the Stock Exchange in the City of London. They were constantly on the phone trying to save or boost up the value of the pound whilst in a state of utter frenzy. They were working perhaps 10 hours a day on constant adrenalin. Under those conditions day in, day out, it was not that surprising that quite a few had a heart attack by the time they were in their mid-thirties.

But we must remember that a certain amount of stress is actually good for us. If we had no stress at all in our lives, then we wouldn't get out of bed in the morning. It is the force that 'revs up' the body and keeps us moving by producing performance-enhancing chemicals like adrenalin and cortisol. This heightens ability in the short term. But this can be applied to tennis as well. Every time we hit the ball, we are placing our bodies under a small amount of stress. When we have to make a decision on whether to go for a shot or hold back, we are placing ourselves under some degree of stress. But this is O.K. If we didn't have any stress at all, we wouldn't even be able to pick up the racquet.

Stress is basically experiencing something that we don't enjoy or relish. When we feel under pressure in tennis we begin to feel stressed out and our enjoyment of the game starts to go out of the window. Pressure can affect all tennis players no matter whether they are a club player or the top players in the world. When I feel under pressure during a match, I can sometimes forget the technique I would normally use if I were relaxed. Once, I went through a period where I forgot the technique I would normally use to hit my second serve. Because of this, I hit many more double faults than usual. This lasted for several weeks. It was very strange.

This pressure sometimes affects other shots in my game as well, because my mind and body have forgotten the technique. So when I try to be positive, I am more likely to hit the ball long or into the net. Because I have lost the technique, I have also lost the feel for the shot. For example, on my forehand side I will play the ball closer to my body, as I subconsciously feel safer doing so. Also, during a rally, if the ball seems a long way off, I tend to over-compensate and so by the time I end up playing the shot, I am virtually on top of the ball. This proves that footwork can also be affected by pressure as well. And because I am playing the ball closer to my body, I am tending to hit it higher over the net and brushing up the back of the ball rather than hitting through it. What I love to do is hit flat forehands that skim the net and stay low after they bounce. But if I'm not confident, it is very hard to rediscover the technique that enables me to hit the ball flat. I can try, but if the technique and feel for the shot are not there, it is likely to go into the net or out. Of course, it does help if your opponent hits a low ball, as to hit a flat ball off a loopy ball is quite tricky.

On my backhand side, I find that I push at the ball rather than hitting through it. My lack of confidence manifests itself in stabbing at the ball with no noticeable follow through. One of my favourite shots is to hit a backhand down the line, especially from a fast first serve. But if I am not at the top of my game, I forget to plant my right foot down and use it as a pivot from which I swing round and through the ball. This gives the shot more power. Instead, I will get my feet stuck and end up not hitting through the ball. This usually results in imparting unintentional sidespin, making the ball go wide of the tramlines.

Good groundstrokes in tennis require good timing. The same is true with the volley. Perhaps even more so, especially when playing doubles. I find that my timing with volley's is affected whilst under pressure and so is the reaction time. Sometimes you have little time to react and so you will either dump the volley into the net or play a very safe volley, giving your opponent a second bite at the cherry.

When you are under pressure, it not only affects your shots, but it also affects your creativity. For when a player is relaxed, he is more likely to play the delicate touch shots. He will place the ball better, go for more acute angles, and try drop shots, stop volleys and angled volleys. These shots need a lot of touch and feel and you are much more likely to pull them off if you are settled and in the right frame of mind.

Pressure can also affect players at various stages of the match. It is usually around an important point or game. For example, a player may be 40-0 up in a game and then lose the next 4 points to go advantage down. He is under pressure now to save the game that he felt he should have won some time ago. He now feels that he should play a special shot to redeem the situation, which only causes him to apply even more pressure on himself.

Perhaps the most well- known scenario is when a player chokes. This is when they are heading for certain victory, start to have thoughts about winning, and then realise they have still got a few more games to get through and so start to panic. The most classic example of this was when Jana Novotna played Steffi Graf in — I believe it was — the 1993 Wimbledon final. It was the final set and Novotna was 5-1 up and coasting towards what seemed like certain victory. For some reason she tightened up and lost the next six games and with it the match. It was embarrassing to watch and I'm sure we can remember when she wept on the shoulder of the Duchess of Kent. I think we all felt for her that day, thinking about what might have been.

So, this pressure can affect any player at any level. Even the greats are not immune to it. But they seem to deal with it best, which is why they are the world's best players. But even at club level, I believe we can do something to lessen the effect of playing under pressure. It's the nature of the beast whether we like it or not. So what can we do to overcome it? Perhaps we should just try to rise above it, or maybe adjust our mental focus. What I shall talk about in the next chapter might just help.

CHAPTER 4
How we can tackle pressure

So far, I have spoken about the focus of playing well rather than winning. This takes the pressure off which we ourselves create. Of course, we all play to win. But should we play tennis to enjoy a win as a single entity, as if we only look forward to the end result of winning, or do we play tennis simply because we enjoy playing the game, win or lose? I believe that the journey can often be more important than the end result. My philosophy is that I would rather lose playing well, than to win playing badly. Again, I believe this helps to take away some of the pressure which is often self-induced. It helps us to pinpoint our focus in the right place. To focus our attention on the tennis rather than on the desired end result, which may or may not come after we have finished the match. It seems daft to project our focus on something that happens afterwards without focusing on what happens before.

I also spoke about effortless play, which happens when we are 'in the zone'. But there is no certainty of it happening. It will happen naturally of its own accord and therefore you cannot force it, or make it happen. It is more likely to happen if you are relaxed, happy and enjoying your tennis, and this is more likely to happen if your focus is in the right area. But as we begin to play well, we place our opponent under greater pressure. As this will usually force our opponent's level of play to go down, so ours will continue to go up and so will our confidence. As our opponent is no longer a threat to us, there is little or no pressure upon us, which gives us a feeling of freedom, creativity and greater confidence. As we continue in this virtuous circle, the game becomes easier and easier and now we are feeling super-confident. It is quite likely that from this point we will slip into that effortless play. For as long as it lasts, we are virtually unbeatable and unstoppable.

But sometimes we are that opponent, when things are not going our way and our opponent is playing great tennis, we just wished we hadn't given him that inch at the start of the match from which his confidence has grown. What has been and gone has happened. The reality is that our opponent is the one applying the pressure and this will happen one day even if we are concentrating on playing well.

So what we need to do is focus on our own game rather than worrying about what our opponent is doing. What we need to do is look at what is most important and then break it down. So, what is more important in tennis, the technique side or the mental side? This question was put to Pat Cash some years ago and he was quoted as saying, "I think technique is more important than the mental side". You can't really argue with a former Wimbledon Champion, but I'm afraid I disagree. I believe that tennis is mental. As I have

32

said, when we are playing well, the winning takes care of itself. So does the technique. Indeed, there are many hackers up and down the country who play unorthodoxly and which cannot and should not be taught from textbooks. But it works for them. My serve, for example, has been classified as a windmill serve, but it works for me and I can usually hit a few aces with it during a match. But what I am saying here is that the technique is sound whilst we are mentally in the right frame of mind. And so when the pressure builds and our positive mental attitude drops, so does our technique and therefore our shot-making. Our technique, therefore, is more dependent upon our mental state of mind rather than the other way round. So the key here is the mental, or the mind, as the mind has tremendous influences on the body, as we have already seen. Of course, all of those parents who have children showing great potential, then it would be advisable to take them to see the local tennis coach. Perhaps your technique needs fine tuning, then yes! Go and see your local tennis coach. But I usually find that most players are happy with their technique when things are going their way. So what we need to concentrate on is the mental side, for our mind is the key.

So now that we have established that the mental side is of greater significance, what we need to know now is, how to maintain a positive mental attitude when we are under pressure.

Imagine the scenario of playing Roger Federer in a match. It almost certainly would never happen to us, but if it did, we would probably be lucky to get a point, let alone a game. Now, supposing he hadn't played for a while and was a bit rusty, maybe even forgotten the technique he used when hitting his cross-court topspin forehand. Then, let's say he was hypnotised and told that he was a terrible tennis player and couldn't play to save his life. If he played us again, probably very little would have changed and he would still thrash us. But supposing he was hypnotised and given the same negative messages, let's say, every two days. As he takes note of these messages, so his level of play would begin to drop and as he himself would realise this, his subconscious would mentally reinforce this. As he was told continuously that he was useless at tennis and experienced the deterioration of his form, it would be reinforced over and over again in his subconscious and so he would believe it more and more until his whole being believed it. What he had been told had become reality because his subconscious mind, which had been told the same negative messages over and over again, had accepted it. The subconscious mind will always act out what it has been told. Of course, it does sound a little far- fetched, but I'm sure you understand the point I am trying to make here. The mind is a very powerful tool and we need to give it positive messages, not negative ones.

I believe that if you tell yourself something consciously you will probably not believe it. But if you keep on repeating the same message to yourself, eventually it will slip down into your subconscious mind. It may take a while, but once your subconscious mind has accepted it, your whole being accepts it and believes it. But this process works with actions as well as with words. For example, when we learn to drive, the driving instructor asks us to put the seatbelt on, check that the gears are in neutral, switch the engine on, then release the hand-brake, then check both mirrors, put the indicator light on and then place one foot on the accelerator and one foot on the clutch, ready to drive off. Eventually, if we keep on doing them, these individual tasks are moulded together to form a pattern of behaviour that becomes automatic. We don't have to think about it. It's the same with tennis. When we are being taught how to hit a serve, we have to plant our feet, then throw up the ball, then back scratch, then hit the ball with follow through. At first it seems hard, as we have to learn each part individually, but eventually we learn to mould them together into one continuous movement and soon the whole movement is registered in the subconscious, ready for the next time. This action should be remembered for the rest of our lives. But we might forget if we don't play very often, or more likely when we come under some pressure, which, rather than forgetting the movement or technique, will probably be compromised.

Our brains are like a huge computer made up of different parts. What goes on in the brain consciously or subconsciously is the mind. In computer terms, the brain is the hardware and the mind is the software. One of these parts of the brain is memory recall. Everything we take in about our world through our senses, consciously or subconsciously, is stored in this part of the brain. If we compared it to a computer, it is made up of thousands if not millions of different files. One of those files stores how to hit your serve, another one how to hit your forehand and another one may be completely different such as the letter that comes after the letter 'k' in the alphabet. But when you come under pressure, the access to that file may become a little more tricky. Indeed, you may have no access to it at all. When we become tense, our minds recognise this and in my case, when I am tense, my mind will only allow access to the file which stores the forehand played under that tension, and indeed a less positive one. This explains that when I am playing with little confidence, I subconsciously hit my forehand closer to my body. But if I begin to play with greater confidence, then my mind will again be able to access the file that remembers how to hit a more positive forehand. So how can we access the file, the more positive file, when we are lacking confidence due to pressure? Let us look at a positive example in human form.

One of the greatest players of all time, and indeed on grass, was Pete Sampras. I always remember watching him at Wimbledon on T.V. In the years that he won the tournament, he would probably only lose his serve three or four times. One of the reasons he lost his serve so few times was because, if he was ever break point down on his serve, serving to the advantage side, he could nearly always hit an ace out -wide. This proves that he must have had a lot of self- belief to do that. Considering that he was under pressure, he was able to access the file from his mind that stores precisely how to hit that serve.

But we can all learn to do that, to hit some of our best shots whilst we are under pressure. Wouldn't it be great? We could win all the big points and with it the match. Unfortunately for me I don't have the fearless mindset that a lot of these young guns have. We both need to instill some discipline into our games, but ironically at each end of the scale. They need to temper their shot-making, especially at pressure points, and tell themselves that they can't always hit winners, and I need to tell myself to go for shots under pressure rather than playing too carefully.

This is the new instruction I shall follow every time I am in a pressure situation. You see, usually I am unable to produce my best tennis in matches. This is partly the reason why I have written this book. To remind myself what I need to do and then to put it into practice. Basically, I want to be a tougher player mentally, to be able to hit good shots under pressure. Not to choke, but to take my opportunities when they come along, especially against a good player. I mean, there is pressure here. You feel you only have one chance to hit a good shot in order to break your opponent's serve. I often think to myself, "shall I go for it with the risk of the ball hitting the net or going out, or shall I play safe? I know, I'll play safe. Oh hell, I've lost the point. I should have been more positive". From now on, I intend to be more positive even if it means losing some matches. For it is better to lose the point thinking positively, than from thinking negatively. Because, in the longer term, it shows our intent and builds our confidence.

It is true that we can play better when we are happy rather than when we are under pressure, lacking confidence and just not feeling as good. I believe what we need to do is to train our minds into believing that, 'I am happy with a bit of pressure, I revel in it and it is a small price to pay for the opportunity to win'. One of my favourite shots is to hit a backhand down the line for a winner off a decent serve out -wide. This makes me feel good, makes me feel happy. Now I want to do that under pressure. I want to be able to access the file from my mind that subconsciously stores how to hit that shot, so that my attitude to pressure changes from something to avoid to something to embrace. To go from not feeling confident about hitting that shot under pressure, to I know I can rely on hitting that shot under pressure. The way I can train myself to do this, I believe, is to take a risk and be positive every time I am in a pressure situation, or lack confidence. When I am happy, I tend to go for winners or bigger shots. I will simply discipline myself to go for it. Of course, it would be easier to play safe, but no! I must go for a positive shot. Because I enjoy going for my shots, I am beginning to replace those negative thoughts with positive ones. Instead of thinking of pressure as a means of subconsciously holding back, I am letting go and I think of it as a time to go for my shots. It will take time, but the more I practice, the more I will get those positive mental muscles into gear. At first, I will probably lose those important points and maybe the match, but if I persevere, I can begin to win those big points and therefore win more matches. With this, I will consciously be thinking about my technique, but that too will get better and better under pressure. In the end, I would have done it so many times under pressure, that it would become a knee-jerk reaction, so that I will hit a big shot without even thinking about it. Now I will be able to access the file where I subconsciously store how to hit that shot.

But we can all teach ourselves to do this. Remember, I said that we can teach our minds through repeating words or sentences via instruction; well we can do the same with repetitive action. Of course, it does sound like I am suggesting we should go out there and play reckless tennis, always going for big shots. No! We should know when to go for a big shot and when to construct the point. Either way, we should feel positive. So, instead of having negative feelings under pressure, we will have positive feelings because we have trained our minds to interpret pressure differently. Look at all the great players and champions of our time. They just seem to have that little extra something, especially when it really matters. This alone makes the difference between winning and losing. Sometimes we will play a player that is better than ourselves, but we find we are staying with them. It's 5-5, and we feel we have got an opportunity to break their serve. There is pressure now because this is the point where we could potentially win or lose the match, but an opportunity for a famous victory. Now we have that self-belief, a positive attitude and a confidence to hit that winning shot necessary to break his serve. In this frame of mind, it is far more achievable, and we are able to select that file from our minds that stores that technique necessary to hit that shot, which we know will win us this very important point. This is what the great players possess. The ability to hit a great shot when it matters, knowing that their technique won't let them down under pressure. This happens because their mind allows them to. Their mind is sound.

I have noticed that in some matches neither player can forge ahead. It goes to 1-1, 2-2, 3-3 and so on. Each player was jostling for position, trying to get the upper hand of his opponent mentally. The one who manages to do so should win the match. The first set was close and won on a tie-break 7-6. In the second set, the player who won the tie-break was mentally on top and had the momentum, and this meant he cruised through the second set and won it 6-1. This happened because the eventual winner possessed greater self-belief, coming from greater positive feelings under pressure. Make sure that person is you.

CHAPTER 5
What are the tactics?

In the last chapter, I dealt with what is most important of all: keeping a positive mental attitude whilst under the chains of pressure. But there are other things we can do as well, before and during a match, that can help our cause. The first one is:-

i) Mental Preparation

What I find really helps me before a singles match is to watch a recording of one of my favourite players and then take the way they play onto the court. I talked a bit about this towards the end of the first chapter. For I find that sometimes my interest in the game is just not there, and so this reduces my motivation and therefore I end up not playing very well. But when I watch my favourite player, especially if he wins, it inspires me to do the same when I get on court. As I said before, what is happening is that we are using the power of visualisation by memorising their shots and their technique and then trying to emulate them. It is a very positive thing as we are focusing our attention on our own game and our technique rather than worrying about our opponent's strengths.

I have to confess that my favourite player of all time and the one who really inspired me was Pete Sampras. This may not come as a great surprise as I have mentioned him several times so far in the book. I just loved the way he played the game; it was a powerful, graceful and well-balanced game that he had. I loved his service action and his flat hitting on the forehand side when he lifted the racquet face and then hit through the ball. His backhand was sometimes a slight weakness but then he was able to produce some stunning winners with it, especially at Wimbledon, where he mainly produced his best tennis. His volleys were the best after Edberg and Rafter and his slam-dunk was legendary. The people who said he was boring I cannot understand. I think they were referring to the fact that his tennis at Wimbledon was too clinical and that he didn't show much emotion compared to other players like Mcenroe and Agassi. But when he wept through the semi-final of the 1995 Australian Open against fellow American Jim Courier, he went from automaton, the tennis machine, to a human being with real feelings. I believe that he was a true professional. He got on with the job and let the racquet do the talking, as he used to put it. And that quarter-final against Alex Corretja in the 1996 U.S. Open was simply unbelievable.

Although Roger Federer has now taken over the mantle that was once Sampras' and may yet prove to be even greater than Sampras was, I do miss not seeing him on the tour anymore. I know it sounds daft, but I always felt as if I knew him, because I could see a lot of my character in him. And yes! I am not ashamed to say he was my idol. For I can say he was the one player who really inspired me and since that time I have modelled my game on his. This inspired me to emulate his style and technique and would help me to have a greater feel for the shot, which is what I want to talk about next.

ii) Feel for the Shot

It is important in tennis to have a feel for the shot. It usually follows on from the technique. Once you have found your own individual technique, the feel for the shot is there and with it control. This control that you now have over the ball gains you the confidence of knowing that you will not miss the shot or make a mistake. But when the technique breaks down under pressure you lose the control meaning that you are less sure about where the ball is going. In this state of mind we feel that we have a small margin of error and this can force us to play safe. But when the feel and control are there, it seems as though we have a much greater margin of error. I find that although this control gives me greater accuracy, I am not trying to hit an exact spot on the court. Rather I am hitting it into an area perhaps 4ft sq. Because I have the technique, I know that the ball will go into that imaginary 4ft sq area. For you instinctively know when you have hit the ball the way you intend to. And you don't have to worry about the angle of the racquet or the timing, your subconscious mind takes care of all that. It's strange to explain but you don't just hit the ball into that 4ft zone, you feel it into that 4ft zone.

iii) Positive Body language

I have talked about it a lot but sometimes during a match, we are going to face some pressure or be in a pressure situation that may result in our level of play dropping. We may simply just not be playing well because it is one of those days, for we can't play well all of the time, it's impossible. But there is something we can do when things are not going our way; we can maintain a positive body language. For if we have a negative body language and shrug our shoulders and say to ourselves, "what can I do", our opponent picks up on this and it feeds them with more and more confidence. And our opponent starts to think to himself, "looks like he's giving up, I reckon I've got this match in the bag". Sometimes in tennis we have to call our opponent's bluff. For example, we could come into the net from a mediocre approach shot, hoping that our opponent will be put off and make a mistake. Or when we are waiting for our opponent to prepare his serve, we could jump up and down or move from side to side to help prepare ourselves and to possibly force our opponent to change the direction of their serve. But all of this helps us to maintain a positive body language. For even if we don't feel like it, by achieving this we are saying to our opponent, "I'm in for the fight and I'm not giving up". Really, it's just play acting, but in the long run it could actually help to turn things around to our advantage. Because by forcing ourselves to be positive in this way, the chances are it will flow into the rest of our game.

iv) Game Plan

As part of our preparation for a match, it is good for us to have a game plan. Some players do not possess any big shots and so they make up for this by being tactically aware, and this comes from experience. Other players know exactly what they want to do on court and so every time they turn up for a match, they bring with them their game A. But if they find that this is not working, they will resort to game B, and if that doesn't work, they may even have a third one.

I think that from reading this book you will realise that there are different ways of playing this game that we call tennis. There are those that go for their shots no matter what the conditions are or what the scoreline stands at. Then at the opposite end of the scale you have the defensive player who gets everything back and who is very successful because of this. Then you have the astute player who doesn't really hit the ball hard but places the ball and keeps his opponent guessing. And finally, you have the player who is a combination of all three and who will play the point according to the scoreline. Now this is my kind of player, an all-rounder with a well-balanced game. This is the game that I like to bring onto the court and one that I shall talk about now along with the tactics involved.

When knocking up with an opponent, especially someone you haven't played before, it is important to spot any weaknesses. Test your opponent's forehand and then refer to his backhand to see if there is a weakness in either wing. Don't forget, you and your opponent will be hitting more groundstrokes than any other shot so it is worth taking some time to see which wing to hit to when an important point is being contested. You might just get a free point.

In tennis, the most important shot is probably the serve. It is the one shot that you have complete control over and the one you can practice by yourself. As this is the case, take the time to develop a good serve, and so when you come to the match, you can keep your opponent guessing by having a variety on both pace and placement. What I sometimes do during a match is serve in one direction for several games and then change the direction whilst still keeping the same ball toss, similar to what Sampras used to do. All of the time you are trying to outwit and out-guess your opponent as the best players are always thinking about what to do next.

In the modern era, the two players that stand out are Sampras and Federer. Both have great all-round games as they can win either from the baseline, especially Federer, or at the net, especially Sampras. In the case of Federer, who I shall use as an example, he doesn't play at 100% capacity throughout the match. Most of the time he is probably at around 80% capacity and then can step it up when he needs to. What I mean by this is that he is not trying to hit the ball as hard as he can on every shot or run every single thing down. He is using his brain and being more selective. Sampras was the absolute master at this. Sometimes, during the earlier stages of a set, he would almost appear uninterested, not running balls down and not trying to break his opponent's serve. But he was so assured on his own delivery that he knew he would not drop his serve. Then at 4-4, say, he would step it up, take his opponent's serve and then win his service game to take the set. He often did this at Wimbledon and proved that his technique would not let him down when it mattered. But coming back to the point of not playing at 100% capacity, you may be thinking that this contrasts with what I was saying in the previous chapter about going for your shots under pressure. The reason why I said that in chapter 4 was that by doing so, we will gradually, over a period of time, change those negative feelings into positive ones. Once you feel confident in that pressure situation, and indeed you may not think of it as pressure anymore, you can then be selective in your shot-making. It was purely to train the mind and not the way we should play all of the time. Of course, there will come a time when we are not feeling confident and it happens to us all; we're only human. At these times it is best not to go for too many shots as we are much more likely to make a mistake. Play the percentages and keep the ball in play.

One of the tactics that I try to establish is to out-manoeuvre my opponent and keep him guessing. Sometimes I will move him from side to side so as to wear him down. Another is to hit out wide several times and then to hit into the open space fairly hard, hoping to get a winner or a weak return which can then be put away on the volley. Yet another good tactic is to go behind your opponent especially when you see him running frantically to cover the open court. It is also effective if you do this on the volley as he will have less time to react. Stefan Edberg did this quite a lot in his matches at Wimbledon. It is important in tennis not to play the same shot too often, and so tactics such as going behind your opponent or playing a drop shot can be used as the surprise elements because your opponent does not expect them.

Another important element in tennis is foot-work. It is something a lot of people don't pay much attention to, and, to their own detriment, gets them into all kinds of trouble. If you can read the ball early or even read the intentions of your opponent, you can sometimes anticipate what he will do so as to get into position early to hit your shot. If you are already in position, you are more likely to hit an attacking shot. If your preparation and footwork are late, you are likely to be hitting the ball defensively.

When our opponent is playing aggressively and is on the attack, it forces us to either go for a big shot, or play defensively. If we take the defensive line, one of the best shots we can play is the lob. If it is a high lob, it will test your opponent's timing on the smash, plus it will give you time to get back into position. As well as this, if the lob is deep enough, it could go down as a winner, so it is a very useful shot to play in defence. The other good defensive shot is the backhand slice. Because you are not hitting through the ball in this shot, you don't have to be directly behind it as you would with a backhand drive, meaning you don't have to run so far to get to it. Also, the spin you impart on the ball helps you to keep control of the shot. If you can keep this shot low as it passes the net, it makes it very difficult for the volleyer. First of all, he has to hit up to get the ball over the net and he also has to hit through the spin. Steffi Graf used this shot a lot to keep her in the rallies, ready to unleash her big forehand.

As I was saying before, it is beneficial to have an all-round game that includes a variety of tactics as well as a variety of shots. When you're up against an attacking player, it is good to sometimes be defensive and other times to be attacking. If your opponent has hit a decent, not a great, but a decent approach shot, then it is probably worth trying to pass him. But if it is an excellent approach shot, it is probably wiser to throw up a lob. Next time he hits a mediocre approach shot, you could choose to lob him. The point I am trying to make is that by changing what you do, you keep your opponent guessing. If you allow him to get into a rhythm or if he sees a pattern of play coming from your racquet, he may start to think that 'if I play this shot, he is going to play that shot'. But by keeping your opponent guessing, you will deny him rhythm, otherwise he will be very difficult to beat.

The last thing I want to say on the subject of tactics and overall game plan and one that you can take with you to every match you will ever play is 'play the ball and not the opponent'. It sounds simple but it is very good advice. This alone condenses several things that I have used many hundreds of words trying to say. It is true that we spend too much time worrying about what our opponent is doing rather than what we are going to do. Every time Roger Federer goes on court, he has a relationship with the ball. Again, it is another area to focus on in aiming to play well. And this takes me right back to chapter 1 when I talked about focusing on playing well rather than winning. By focusing on what we are doing, we are much more likely to be proactive during the rallies than reactive. In the end we should just go out there and enjoy ourselves, remembering that we are lucky to play this great game we call tennis.

Well, I have just about come to the end now but I have enjoyed writing this book and expressing my deeper thoughts about the game. I believe that tennis, just like any other sport, can mirror life, that there are ups and downs in both, and that by learning to be more positive in tennis, may help us to be more positive in our lives. I believe that tennis is a beautiful game, and when I see it as such in my mind, it tends to bring out the creativity in me, allowing me to hit wider angles and giving me the feel to hit drop shots and stop volleys.

Some players are attacking players who like to go for their shots, and others are more defensive and rely on other people's mistakes. I look upon myself as the former because it is more satisfying to win matches through what you have done, rather than what your opponent hasn't done. If you play safe, but your opponent makes too many mistakes and hands you the match, you don't feel as though you've achieved much. But if you have taken the game to your opponent, played some great shots and risen to the challenge when it really matters, I promise you that you'll feel great, that you have achieved something and that you will enjoy your win all the more.

SUMMARY

To summarise, apart from what I have talked about in chapter 5, there are three things that can help us to play better and to win matches. Two of them you have control of and one less so.

You have control in concentrating on playing well rather than winning. This helps you focus on your game and to get the most out of your tennis, rather than focusing on something that hasn't happened yet, or what your opponent is doing. I find that if I play to win, I put more pressure on myself, don't enjoy my tennis so much and probably end up losing. Just go out there, enjoy your tennis, and winning will take care of itself.

You also have control in learning to play better under pressure by replacing the negative thoughts that destroy your technique and crea-tivity, with positive thoughts, by training and fine tuning the mind into believing that pressure brings out the best in you, and is something to embrace. This can be done with repetitiveness, repeatedly going for shots under pressure, until the sub-conscious mind recognises that this is how we will act every time we are in that situation. From then on, we will recognise pressure as a positive thing and go for our shots instinctively, without thinking about it.

The one thing that we have less control of is playing effortlessly when we are 'in the zone'. I believe that when we play in this zone, something remarkable happens. For we don't just tune into ourselves, but we also tune into the spiritual powers that exist beyond the realms of this world. And that is why luck goes our way when this happens, because we are tuned into the spiritual that is at unity with itself, where all things are possible. It is the blueprint to what life is really all about. At the point of becoming one with the spiritual universe, we become who we are meant to be and who we are destined to become. It's just that for most of the time we are disconnected from it.

As I said at the beginning of the book, I believe that tennis is spiritual. Because when we are playing effortless tennis, we are being led by our spiritual selves that have tapped into this power source, which is far greater than the limitations of this world. But when we are not playing at this level, we are turned off from this power source and are being led by our non-spiritual, conscious selves.

Next time you play a tennis match, tell yourself, "I don't have to win this match", and this will take so much pressure off yourself. Now you will be able to play with much more freedom and therefore are much more likely to slip into that 'effortless zone'. When this happens, you not only commune with the spiritual universe, but you ultimately commune with the one who created it.

REFERENCES

Greaves, J. quote, "it's a funny old game".

Only Fools and Horses (1996). Episode 'Time on our Hands' – the Trotter's become millionaires.

S.A.S. motto, 'he who dares, wins'.

Wiseman, R. (2003). The study of luck and good fortune.

Sampras, P. (2000). Quote, "I don't look upon it as pressure but as an opportunity".

Fight/flight response article (2007).
www.helpishere.co.uk/fightflight.html

Body memory recall article (2007).
www.bodymemory.com/freezeresponse.html

Sress management article (2003).
www.stress.org.uk/4617/9903.html

Cash, P. (2000). Quote, "I think technique is more important than the mental side".